THE ADDRESS BOOK

ALSO BY STEVEN HEIGHTON

POETRY
Stalin's Carnival
Foreign Ghosts
The Ecstasy of Skeptics

FICTION
Flight Paths of the Emperor
On earth as it is
The Shadow Boxer

ESSAYS
The Admen Move on Lhasa

ANTHOLOGIES
A Discord of Flags: Canadian Poets Write about the Gulf War
(with Peter Ormshaw & Michael Redhill)
Musings: An Anthology of Greek-Canadian Literature
(with main editor Tess Fragoulis, & Helen Tsiriotakis)

THE ADDRESS BOOK

STEVEN HEIGHTON

POEMS

ANANSI

Published in 2004 by
House of Anansi Press Inc.
110 Spadina Avenue, Suite 801
Toronto, ON, M5V 2K4
Tel. 416-363-4343
Fax 416-363-1017
www.anansi.ca

Distributed in Canada by
Publishers Group Canada
250A Carlton Street
Toronto, ON, M5A 2L1
Tel. 416-934-9900
Toll free order numbers:
Tel. 800-663-5714
Fax 800-565-3770

Distributed in the United States by
Independent Publishers Group
814 North Franklin Street
Chicago, IL 60610
Tel. 800-888-4741
Fax 312-337-5985

08 07 06 05 04   1 2 3 4 5

NATIONAL LIBRARY OF CANADA CATALOGUING IN PUBLICATION DATA

Heighton, Steven, 1961–
The address book / Steven Heighton.

Poems.
ISBN 0-88784-698-X

I. Title.

PS8565.E451A64 2004   C811'.54   C2004-900770-X

Cover design: Bill Douglas at The Bang
Front cover photograph: Nancy Friedland
Author photograph: Neil Graham
Typesetting: Brian Panhuyzen

Canada Council
for the Arts

Conseil des Arts
du Canada

ONTARIO ARTS COUNCIL
CONSEIL DES ARTS DE L'ONTARIO

*We acknowledge for their financial support of our publishing program the
Canada Council for the Arts, the Ontario Arts Council, and the Government of
Canada through the Book Publishing Industry Development Program (BPIDP).*

Printed and bound in Canada

Lambie George Stephanopoulos (1937–2001)

Εις μνήμην

Contents

IV FIFTEEN APPROXIMATIONS

For everyone
The swimmer's moment at the whirlpool comes

— Margaret Avison

I loved so many people everywhere I went —
Some too much, others not enough.

— Woody Guthrie

THE ADDRESS BOOK

I

FOURTEEN ADDRESSES

ADDRESS BOOK

Bad luck, it's said, to enter your own name
and numbers in the new address book.
All the same, as you slowly comb
through the old one for things to pick

out and transfer, you are tempted to coin
yourself a sparkling new address,
new name, befitting the freshness of this clean-
slating, this brisk kiss

so long to the heart-renders — every friend
you buried or let drift, those Home for the Aged
maiden relations, who never raged
against the dying of anything, and in the end

just died. An end to the casualties pressed
randomly between pages — smudged, scribbled chits
with lost names, business cards with their faded
bold fronts of confidence, solvency. The palimpsest

time made of each page; the hypocrite it made
of you. Annie, whom you tried two years to love
because she was straight-hearted, lively, and in love
with you (but no strong-arming your cells and blood);

Mad Carl, who typed poet-to-poet squibs in the pseudo-
hickish, hectoring style of Pound, all sermonfire
and block caps, as AINT FIBRE ENOUGH HERE, BOYO,
BACK TO THE OLE FLAX FIELD . . . this *re* a score

of your nature poems. When he finally vanished
into the Far East, you didn't mind the silence.
Still, this guilt, as if it weighs in the balance,
every choice — as if each time your pen banished

a name it must be sensed somewhere, a ballpoint stab, hex-
needle to the heart, the treacherous
innocent *no* of Peter, every X
on the page a turncoat kiss. . . .

Bad luck, it's said, to enter your own name in the new
book — as if, years on, in the next culling,
an executor will be leafing through and calling
or sending word to every name but you.

CASHING OUT: FROM A LETTER

— waiting our way through school at townie restaurants
or the Banff Springs, and every midnight, shift's end,
beat but abuzz, we'd have to run through accounts
as if for our own small firm; make it all balance and
keep what remained. Wallets crammed with that fresh cash —
blue fins, red deuces — were good to feel, to squander,
a big man in the small hours, but, looking back, *that* rush
wasn't best. Best was cashing out itself, the ledger

shut, shift squared — how that neat, nightly closure
freed us to dream and idle, live by the moment, no
bills in bales, waiting wills to sign, roofers to humour;
address books lost online. You live now on a warmer shore
and you're loaded. But think back when we didn't own or owe —
no clerk to life's complications — not even a letter.

THE AMERICAN NIGHT LISTENS

His longing, strung on the American night, knew its own slavage.
Debt peon to such lean solitudes. *Drink with me, please.*
Precious friend, you cannibal of elders, your maimed
shoes, lager-lame step, made a hundred-storied ledge
of any sidewalk: hesitation-cut cracks. Forgive me this
going. I always miss you. You thought your uncombed
thoughts and spoke them, penned dense letters so
manically amped and you still must, I guess,
for others somewhere. We two in the post-party
dark as MacGowran does *Malone Dies*, and the lines
of stereo lights are a landing field below, blinking red
in fog. How your mind then seemed a soaring lamp.
Tell me something important, you said (drunk, dead
drunk again), and I was stumped. Friend, I still am.

THE WOOD OF HALFWAY THROUGH

A daughter

Any forest craves torrents
of breeze in noon's steeper blaze: as a glider
seeks thermals coiled into high currents,
each aerial a ladder

into middle air. Appearance
never speaks for marrow. I think I was sadder
before you than friends saw. Now all my *aren'ts*
and *shouldn'ts* recede, I'm the reader

of a tongue lacking the negative mood,
the conditional, and other places to hide.
Who is it loves you, his heart now a lantern

in the dark wood of halfway through? The one
you made solid when he felt himself shade,
who made his way back from the border, made good.

CONSTELLATIONS

After bedtime the child climbed on her dresser
and peeled phosphorescent stars off the sloped
gable-wall, dimming the night vault of her ceiling
like a haze or the interfering glow
of a great city, small hands anticipating
eons as they raided the playful patterns
her father had mapped for her — black holes now
where the raised thumb-stubs and ears of the Bat
had been, the feet of the Turtle, wakeful
eyes of the Mourning Dove. She stuck those paper
stars on herself. One on each foot, the backs
of her hands, navel, tip of nose and so on,
then turned on the lamp by her bed and stood close
like a child chilled after a winter bath
pressed up to an air duct or a radiator
until those paper stars absorbed more light
than they could hold. Then turned off the lamp,
walked out into the dark hallway and called.

Her father came up. He heard her breathing
as he clomped upstairs preoccupied, wrenched
out of a rented film just now taking grip
on him and the child's mother, his day-end
bottle of beer set carefully on the stairs,
marking the trail back down into that evening
adult world — he could hear her breathing (or
really, more an anxious, breathy giggle) but
couldn't see her, then in the hallway stopped,
mind spinning to sort the apparition
of fireflies hovering ahead, till he sensed
his daughter and heard in her breathing
the pent, grave concentration of her pose,
mapped onto the star chart of the darkness,
arms stretched high, head back, one foot slightly raised —
the Dancer, he supposed, and all his love
spun to centre with crushing force, to find her

momentarily fixed, as unchanging
as he and her mother must seem to her,
and the way the stars are; as if the stars are.

2001, AN ELEGY

First scene

       I was the child
plucked from Miss Porch's kiln of a second grade
classroom, Indian summer 1968, the getaway Datsun
panting at the curb, Dad at the wheel — and you, like Jackie O,
with gangland shades and auburn bouffant, gold
drachma profile, making me your merry truant,
secret suitor. And for a matinee. (Miss Porch,
I think, subsequently disapproved.)
Decades later you would recall nothing of this,
and then, at the closing, nothing at all.
But the film lingers. How HAL's robotic voice
resembled Vice Principal Hoop's ominous monotone,
Just what do you think you're doing . . . Dave . . .
and the spacemen in their plastic hibernacula
as futuristic pharaohs, LIFE FUNCTIONS
TERMINATED . . . and how, for thirty-three years,
that science-fiction date "2001" reared, monolithic
though distant as Jupiter, black parsec-stone or
postmodern tower, where I'd make it
to forty years, my parents
a Paleolithic sixty-five.

Later scene

       The deep space of Mount Pleasant
Theatre smudged with sweet, unfamiliar fumes
(unlike the Pall Malls you're smoking) and I press close,
peer up as Kubrick's chromatic vortices make violent
kaleidoscopes of your cat-eye lenses, the capsule
like a pill plummets through psychedelic voids, and
you and Dad (I think now) wonder if maybe
Fantasia would have been better. . . . Now see the hero,

retired, sexless, mummified in his final bed —
hard to conceive, from inside the living
frame of family, such mythic age,
and solitude. There are losses beyond losing.
The one closing I never foresaw:
that 2001 would be your year to leave, and me
in the "dark wood" of halfway through, commuting
fear to fear, until I reach your cribside (yes,
just that) and recite — since hearing's always last
to lapse — your favourite Hopkins — *I desired to go*
where springs not fail, where flies no . . .

Cotside. Coffinside. *Wait for me wait for me*
wait for me the widower said —

Closing scene

                    Bed in a white room
where I sit by your side for a last *again*, read you more,
No sharp and sided hail, and a few lilies blow.
From a lampless house in high-flung fallow
you've the metropolis for starfields, high beams
of cars on concession roads cruising slow
and straight as satellites, space probes.
                                        In New Year's
smallest hours, you do hear a child deep inside
your ear, murmuring, *Mama,*
listen. It's 2001.
We made it.

SWIMMER IN THE AVALANCHE

. . . caught in an avalanche, your only hope is to literally swim with the current of the slide. When the snow is still in a kind of liquid state and going up to 200 km per hour, it's possible to move in it. By struggling like a swimmer in rapids you may be able to reach the surface and stay there, or close to it. So when the movement ends, those tons of snow turn to concrete and the "breath-mask" starts to crystallize and choke you, you're within reach of help.

— Mountain guide, *Aspen Gleaner*, December 2002

Caught in the chute's
thundering tonnage you're struck
that this is how time moves:
no stoic flow, no old man river, but
the ruck and tumult of seismic tides, Niagaras
burying your barrel into the sinkpool as
now, in the snow, you're threshing with silent
semi-comic limbs: sped-up and footless
follies in the sluice, slapstick, a cartoon
loser run through the wash, but here no promise
of weekly revival, in your flux of common trials
(pallbearer's shoulder, the knock of the auditor)
gaining gravity though always with back-swirling
second thoughts, nostalgic arabesques, all
ripping your self crossways, like desire — you
shooting like a loose ski through the clear-cut
wood of halfway, even landmark boulders
enrolled now in the general skelter,
and this is a life
or its marrow:
                        no surface drama like a climber, arc-lit
channel swimmer, yet swimming all the same
down there, fighting upward, you hope upward,

through the whiteout span until
stasis makes you final:
                        face cramped to a mask, in a morgue
of remorse and small habits, or
snow-cauled, thrust from your chrysalis
into sunlight, the gentian wind
of the pinnacles, within reach again of hands,
wearing your own face now,
and standing ——

MIXED TAPES

They almost ask for musical backing, some feelings,
or even to be sung, but since life (you know this)
isn't opera, and your all-too-spoken arias
are prey to mundane upstaging, missteps
of the tongue, you pick tracks of singers scattered
in time, and temper — yet bound by the way
they overheard your heart, and pinched
its unformed lines — and you record them
in skewed new orders:
                    Nick Drake opening for Nina Simone,
John Prine in bed with Edith Piaf,
and later, languid and alone, tragic smoker
under a Gatsby-green light, on a summertime pier. . . .
No, you choose the name.

You know how clichés, the same
you'd never leave in a poem, that would shame you
breathed into a mouthpiece, are disguised
somehow — or are they renewed, justified
by the right tune? *Still missing you.*
Keep kissing you.
Maybe that's what a tune is for. Maybe
it's why you burn mixed disks, make tapes
in hi-fi, normal bias — 60 to 90 minutes
is best; no rushed declarations of love.
You'll sit up with a bottle of something red,
a tape deck, and this clichéd, constant
aching, to reclaim lines you mean so deeply
they must be your own.

With this kiss my life begins.

You're not alone, anymore.

FROM A HIGH WINDOW

There was no night in that night.
The moon soldiered through the smog.
The rails so near your bedside window
you both smelled the cigarettes of engineers
with diesel drafts, steel wheels stammering
the last, brakes-on stage to the port, shaking
the bedframe, swivelling ambulance strobes
across your ceiling.
                        He tells you that he used to love
being the one who loves less. Believe him,
leave on the lamp. Let tired trainmen wonder
why it burns so late, in a blue window, crepe
curtains alive there like a negligee drying
in the crude breath of engines arriving from the east.
(They haul sunrise behind them out of the Rockies,
a whole dry summer in their cars.)
Don't let him doze. Lie to him
that this, and he, are the only best, tonight
in your boxcar of a room, floating
high over the sleepers on their bed of stones,
where you both out-sing the trains.

LOST WATERFALLS

For the strangled impulse there is no redemption
— Patrick Kavanagh

There was a waterfall, mapped in the founding
survey, two hundred years ago and lost,
eroded — something — so no later crew,
miner, or bushwalker has seen a thing.
                            The river
it should have ruptured is still there, unspooling
where it ought to, out of the Burnt Hills down through timber
east of the Perth Road, chattering with chipped
fossils, flint shards sparked by eels, then pooling
in a colonnade of cedars where the lost
falls should be exploding, still.

Went looking for you, what I thought was you.
A skirling of wind in the skymost branches
and peering round me for the radiant detonation,
vapours pulsing up from the sinkpool, I seem
to see the chalk-white shock of it — a cliffslide
through the cedars' warped, ashen balusters —
almost feeling the mist of this vision
condensed to a strange dew's
trickle down my face.

Wind dwindles then, dies, and that ghost-foam
flickers, the cataract roar ebbs to the dodder
of a stone-bald, greying, oblivious river,
and I go.

Where have you got to? Gone to. Two hundred years,
the path healed over, the cedars deadfallen

or deeper in the sky, the mapmakers
deeper in the ground.
                    There is a waterfall, they lied,
afraid that love dries to a dotted line
on the map, that the river in time
slips underground, and   *This to prove*
we were loved. This whim
against what drifts to dark.

We know, of course, it will not be found.

MISSING FACT

> Noli me tangere, *for Caesars I ame;*
> *And wylde for to hold, though I seeme tame.*
> > — Thomas Wyatt, c. 1535

Sometimes time turns perfect rhyme to slant,
as in Wyatt's famous sonnet — how the couplet
no longer chimes, his "ame" turned "am," now coupled
more by pattern, form. So everything gets bent
and tuned by time's tectonic slippage. You and
I, for instance, no longer click or chord
the sharp way we did, when secretly wired
two decades back (not fifty — but then human
prosody shifts faster); and surely that's best —
half-rhyme better suits the human, and consonance,
not a flawless fit, is mostly what counts
over years. But, still, this urge (from the past?
our genes?) to shirk all, for one more perfect-
coupling rhyme: for two again as one pure fact.

DRUNK JUDGEMENT

A night address

The world is wasted on you. Show us one clear time
beyond childhood (or the bottle) you spent your *whole*
self — hoarding no blood bank backup, some future aim
to fuel — or let yourself look foolish in reckless style
on barstool, backstreet or dancefloor, without a dim
image of your hamming hobbling you the whole while.
Voyeur to your own couplings, you never did come
with them, did you, even when you did? You said Hell
is details, when Hell was just the cave, the concave-
mirrored skull you dwelt inside, your left hand
polishing while the other shook to clinch a deal —
Provide, provide! Sure, in the end, like any soul
you were endless *and yets* — brave, deft with phrases, kind —
three cheers for you. Too closed to want what others love
you vetoed life —

      were there other worlds to crave?

THE BODY SURFERS

Two of us in the funnelling grooves, brief graves
scooped between waves when seas pumped from the pine
coast of Honshu hammer Long Beach, hack at the cove's

Bocce-ball seabreak, and us in the fast lane
outbound with an offshore rip, like leaves
blown out of reach of land, willingly. With wine

ashore waiting and wet-suit secure, soaring
beachward on the afterthoughts of seisms
six thousand sea miles behind, we were jeering

at the hunched grocer in the soul, all truisms,
tax forms, fridge magnet lists of those miring
Must Do's. Each crest's climactic spume held prisms

through which the beached life ashore was at last
plainly seen — so now finally the great change
would have to come. Then somehow we were out past

breakers in breathing groundswell, bound out of range
of help, hadn't noticed the undercover, west-
smuggling rip now slipping us past that vast henge

of mossed, guanoed sea rock, like the last custom
post of the familiar world. In any myth
this moment comes. You yelled warnings, panic swam

visibly over you, you knowing the depth
and the distance and thrashing hard to get home,
in your heart already pledging a fresh oath

of allegiance to the mundane and the "normal,"
in all their tedium and miracle, their slighted,
shy radiance, while over me something else fell

tacitly: a storm-calm, as if I'd waited
lifetimes for this swimmer's moment, or arrival
at a crux I'd somehow invited — created? —

and the one-way drift translating me further
so the surf's slamming and surfers' cries receded
with the foam-flash on the combers' peaks like lather

until (as if mind, or heart, had righted
in muddling seas) I snapped clear of whatever
still held me — woke to fear as if the frigid

swell were inside me, filling my guts. And sculled
homeward, hard, with numb hands. Close moments and we were
beached with the bull-kelp, laughing as breakers scrolled

home around us — ovation to a guys' tale, another
taproom anecdote — but not the story I might
once have told (a boast disguised as a story) —

How cool I was under fire. No. That unthinking fear
you showed? Just love for the shore. And not a heartbeat
of doubt. You're the final hero of my story.

TOURISTS IN ISTANBUL

Her skullcap, a small dome of white muslin
filigree, upstaged Hagia Sophia's fabled,
dazing inner altitudes, where pigeon,
dove, garbage tern and the shadows of hidden
restorers, high on a hatchwork Babel

of scaffolding, thronged. The cardiac thrum
of wings an epoch above in the dome
as she passes, eyes understandably upturned,
the way the artists, working stupors, planned
to have it — and I'm at odds with their dream,

competing for her gaze, vainly willing
it down to mine, in the "Church of the Divine
Wisdom," as she with her breeze of passing
body, bare limbs and white skullcap, spilling
bonds of hair, grips and holds me to the human.

II

GRAVESONGS

*Death is accorded no belief, & old friends
are constantly expected*

— Milton Acorn

THE PHONE NEVER RANG

— like the silence of a friend with information
you know concerns you; that stubborn secrecy.
On many days one is written to by no one,
the door never unlocked. When Maurice Chevalier

finally cancelled his own conscious posterity
with an *apéritif* of pills, his manservant
(he had one, of course) was put on record by
a few papers: "Monsieur, he almost went

mad, waiting, wishing still to be cast. Small parts,
even! The phone never rang." *Every little breeze*
seems to whisper Louise. And how, as one sits
with a body after the blood's setting, in these

dens filling with dusk (where no one thinks of a lamp),
something old in each mourner still awaits a sigh
as lips end-rhyme some posthumous insight, hint
from a locked locale. . . . Think how Houdini,

dying, said, "Wait by my grave, Bess. If I can, I'm
going to reach you — though I suppose that's no safe
bet . . ." But then it's a given, the Silence of the Tomb —
the silence of the living brings deeper grief.

"Satchel Feet," the giant Primo Carnera — go ask
him, who never knew the mob bought him his title,
who withered from world champion to asterisk
in a bell's knelling, who from his hospital

deathbed told a last, bored stringer for the *Tribune,*
"I haven't a friend in the world." Or Abishag,
ex-stroker of all King David's crowns, now a crone
in the frost, swabbing steps with pail and rag —

she must have wondered why the palace never rang.
And last, Tom, my friend, his books being forgotten
without malice, cold or casual — without even
our awareness — on your floor that last evening

as cicadas whined beyond like wires, skateboard boys
clattered hard, and you helpless to rise, realizing
this event, too, would not be pillowed by praise —
how only friendship ever lessened the blows —

you must have wondered why your phone didn't ring.

MAPS OF THE TOP OF THE WORLD

New moon — a starveling
  curled on blue earth and quickly
    swallowed by snowdrift clouds —

Late in *The Lure of the Labrador Wilds*
the solemn falling of snow in the firwood, the
famine-wood, and before long sly, soft winds
till drifts oversift the tomb of the tent
like an A-frame in a snowbelt storm

— and inside that canvas husk
a smaller husk, now exempt from struggle, the ardent
anomalies of consciousness, animal heat
and shunted blood. Sink now sleep a fugue
of crackling maps, wistful misnamings echoing
in talus-grey defiles —
                    Providence Point
                    Cape Homer
                    Homeward Cove —
                                        of firepits
once more warmly
antlered with flame.

                    The explorer's dream
is just the yearning of doomed
molecules for eternity, ancient urge
to impregnate barrens with menhirs,
cairns and runes, with
ruins,

          and you there likewise,
                    Purdy,
in your oxygen tent,
              mind off elsewhere
                          stumbling in a blizzard
of drugs —

                    you too came this far,
imprinted the ice shelves and foolscap floes
of how many blank sheets
and pharmacy notebooks,
                    wanted to "do the country"
so you kept afoot, always moving
against the stasis to come, always
talking back at the silence to come

                    and at that final forecloser,
repossessor, who serves the body
such intimate writs, gives pressing notice
that each breath is borrowed, the warmed and
wobbling space you occupy
is leased —

And maybe all this movement and exploration is really
in hopes of finding — founding — some new "Vinland
the Good"
                    somewhere out beyond
all vital eviction, where poets, friends,
like dogged squatters in life's rickety A-frame,
vie and recite over homebrew, wild grape wine,
with invincible livers on a pine-box patio
that never will sag further than this

— and the day holds, hovering at the late August hour
of light's most inebriate angle, on the relic
phonograph Paul Robeson revived to the lap
and backbeat of lake waves, woodwind breezes
through the weeping willow's green marquee,
and the old rowboat is straked and caulked so that later
a few might row it across to the brook mouth
and alongside the pioneer graveyard, knowing
its bottomless appetite is finally sated
and the living forever barred. . . .

He loved the poetry of place-names most
and set them down accordingly —

So sink now sleep a fugue
of crackling maps, wistful misnamings
signposted in permafrost

> Ft Good Hope
> Mt Somerset
> Pt Victory

the pit of the belly
once again warmly
furnaced with flame,

and "know where the words came from"

THE LAST LIVING SPEAKER OF THE ERONDHA TONGUE
CAUGHT ON VIDEO A FEW HOURS BEFORE HER DEATH

Her pauses lengthening, the abyss
between phrases like the faults between
a heart's ragged, forceless
beating on an

ECG. A fickle
flickery line that seems to chart
the country of her people —
its tablelands, tors, inert

streambeds and saltwaste
cratered round. Except that the bone-
sown soil was never the ghost-
green of this electric line,

its vital tines now fainter, fewer.
Is she revisiting that flower
said to blossom a single night
per century? They knew where to wait

and why. Mind-mapped each chant-line,
glyph-line of bluffs where outback
and ocean collide, two deserts, rock
to reef; knew rain

as reluctant manna. (I know noble
savagery is bogus —
I *like* my wires, my digital sonatas,
laptop and remote. But in the rubble

of her failing words something
of me too lies unaddressed. Song
by song, cell by cell, the dying
take galaxies along

with them into the grave — or
should. She does. Any death,
I used to feel, has to cancel a star
from the canopy, and with

all its satellites; but what of me, us,
of this manic, fractured consciousness?
This at least we should have
the right to know before we leave,

that dying we deprive the world
of something whole. What is it I killed
that gnaws me now? What did you wall
away still murmuring? Fallout, ash in the well;

I know a desert when I'm in one.) Soon
her eyes will pool with the ceiling's
grey pasteboard overcast, the uncoilings
of soul into circuitry done,

and now for eulogy what I need
most is to goad my*self*, soul
corroded by years of trivial
discourse, data, to praise — a shade

re-fleshing body and senses through
spells of deep song: this tongue too
is a moment of moistened dust, of breath,
and each death's a fierce urging, though

hers most of all: a death within a death.

ENGLISH CEMETERY, GASPÉSIE

In a corner of the yard, quiet
And discreetly removed from worn, grey-
Shouldered monuments, you find the least
Ancient headstones weathering uneasily
On the lip of a seacliff. Giving onto the gulf
And east winds, these smaller markers glow
White as sails in the sun's offing; lean in the gust
Like fishermen over a deck's edge. On the brink
Of a shrinking headland, stripped willows
Hunch and quaver.
                                Even the clearest of the stones
Seem to list into whispering
sallow earth, *Sacred*
To the Heart of Susannah Jane Tom Sommers
is laid here, and John Francis Mahon, who
Died on the Magdalen River 1910 and left
no one behind
                    (except
perhaps the inscriber —)

Other stones are not so easy to read.
Just seventy years have sanded them,
salted them white until
now in the annulling sunlight
they are wholly illegible — runes
in an abandoned tongue,
ideas on a blank slate —

but someone must have carved them
once, cracked them in stone
with strong hands and Anglican assurance believing
they would endure for centuries

The yard however is empty at my visit —
no English speakers live
so far east now
their last words engraved years ago

                      And lying among them somewhere
the scribe, a nameless sexton
who did double duty with chisel and spade
the last of his enclave
to die perhaps
wondering in the end
who would keep the lawn trimmed
who polish and clean the stones

aware at his last sigh
of a mute wind
hammering the walls

FROM THE LOST DIARY

2 Jan. 1912: 87° 20' 8" S., 160° 40' 53" E.

At first the sound was like a raw stropping
of steel on steel although we had little
such heavy stuff along. Or one of the men
once more adoze in the traces whimpering
in waking nightmare but no it was too loud
and instantly repeated and then somebody
halloed There! a catamaran shadow
against the low sun hovering, and now
above us banking sheer and screeching came
a gaunt monstrous skua, first animate
thing we had seen save for one another
and our lost ponies since starting onto
the ice shelf at the sea two months ago.
Half blind, rused by the loomings and the ridged
snow in spars like candlerock, defiling
through gin-cold ventricles of ice and back
into eye-stabbing sunlight — if alone
I'd have feared for my own mind not the gull's.
Yet we all did see it. And not so little
food as a colony of lichen or a louse
for eight hundred miles. How many days' flight
would that need? It did look starved. S believed
some disturbance in the upper atmosphere
must have veered the bird far off range and yet
the high cirrus had sat unconvulsed for days.
And here it was not a hundred and fifty
miles from the Pole. Somebody quipped about it
beating us there and the Norwegians too
while the snow-bellied bird touched down ahead
and fluttered always a few yards farther
as we neared and at this, what, this rumour
or fledged missive dispatched by the dream world
of warm yearning life to ourselves a brief
agony of delight punctured the frozen

shell of our shambling fatigue, fear, hunger,
frostburn and returned to us our purpose.
All agreed the visitation was an auspice.
The messenger would see us to the Pole.
Yet I wondered still what she was doing
so remote from her own skies in that time —
not quite an hour — till she flared her wings and rose
with serum-yellow eye unclosing to swerve
close above us in the return direction,
diminishing then dipping out of view
as a bead of mercury in the day's bitter
foregone ——

THE LAST GREENLANDER

A number of writers, including Ingstad, have speculated that the man might have been the last Norse Greenlander to perish, basing this conjecture on his unburied condition in the inner hallway, the horribly squalid state of the farmstead in which he fell, and the chronology, which puts his death around 1500 A.D. — the supposed approximate date of Austerbyggd's extinction.
— Gudrun Audun, *Death in Greenland*

I dreamed you as the last one, father,
your shattered skeleton
fanned out and massive, a burnt-out Orion
sunk in the black turf floor of the corridor

where you collapsed, and the archaeologists
found you, four centuries late. The hall's too narrow,
a slapdash coffin, where you lie prone, with wrists
uncrossed, limbs splayed, as if you burrow

down tunnels of ice, or swim
channels to the light of the vital opening
you never reach. Stillborn father; always lying
eyes merged into clay, concealed — in dream

you never will turn, face-on, to me. So I linger
over the delicate archipelago
that bones of feet and toes have mapped, each finger,
the mossed, rusted prop of the pelvis, till somehow

I see you back alive — gaunt-jawed, handsome
and baffled — whatever was yours
you've had to bury, so now you haunt pastures,
byres, the hearth-hall life once warmed, or roam

home fields blistered with a pox of shallow
grave-pits, till in grief and shame you thrust
back inside, fling open the bed-closet doors to
set hands on whoever must

still be there, malingering. Living! Your eyes pure pupils
in the early dark — you always must
be up while others sleep, you always would protest
the reticence of God. And the grim tabernacles

where we outslept famine lie empty, swept clean,
of course — so long as your limbs still
grasped the exacting grammar of your will
you'd have kept all things in trim, the Green-

landic hymns hummed each Sabbath, hearth fed,
the hours of waking, labour, and sleep
duly meted. And long after all hope
has tallowed out, your head, tonsured with age, still bowed

over an empty trencher. At heart a pastor
though your hands are hard; I see my grave was the last
you laboured and prayed over, clay cradle in permafrost
at the foot of the ice sheet, hours over Auster-

byggd, the grievous, unyielding
acres and the sprawl
of roofless, corbelled chambers where they'll
find you, generations late. Now dreaming

of that dig, father, I find you too — last to fall,
they'll say, though it won't be proved —
pulled down by the weight you bore too well,
alone in the end (as you were before),
                                        but loved.

A PERISHABLE ART

I found my mother's footprints in the snow
still fresh, she'd passed this way only moments before.
Her tracks climbed and crossed the treeless hills at the skyline.
Her heels were half-moon gouges in the white crust, glowing.

The prints held no warmth. Their shapes already changing.
Surprising how directly she had managed
to shear through that wandering terrain, as if
something unusual in the wind-empty range

of hills had captured her eye and drawn her on
with a purpose. And in fact all the signs there were
pointed to this — the long intervals between prints
suggesting haste, their unfaltering

evenness betraying a certain intensity, a certain
determination. I followed them some distance, saw nothing
but blue sky white hills and shadows between hills
and the prints themselves receding, as if by plan

clean as a survey trail or concession road. . . .
Before dark it grew windy. Powder snow
rippled like gauze curtains between hills, and quickly
filled in footprints — mine behind me
                                        and my mother's before.

ABOVE DAWSON

Dusk, in autumn woods —
  hoarding Arctic cranberries,
    capsules of setting sunlight.

GRAVESONG

Jan. 02

It's said that the dead want us worthy of something.
Why do you wait till the waiting fills years?
Pain shovelled deep has no chance to bloom open.
A grave, a stringless guitar, a lost song.

Enough. They must hate to see us here sleeping.
Why will you stall till the stalling's your life?
It's wake yourself now or never be woken.
Lifetimes you waited for the right phone to ring.

The drowned, it was said, could be heard at night singing.
Why do you never set out while you can?
It's fix yourself now or always be broken.
A grave, a stringless guitar, a last song.

III

ULTRASOUND

BLACKJACK

Hit: to take another card, and risk breaking.
Stand: to stick with what you have.

The dealer is dailiness, and the asking —
hit or stand? — comes more often than you guess.
Missed cues can fill a life. Or you signal wrong,

the house responds, no recourse. Standing with less
may be safer — you know the odds — but even then
the temptation is to hit. Sometimes loss

at long odds looks better than a sure win;
as if winning were a sure thing, ever.
In some dreams a familiar house will open

into unsuspected rooms, door after door
glides ajar, yet you hang back and consciousness
cuts in like an eviction. But what if you were

not so anxious to wake back into your less
uncharted life, and chanced those farther rooms . . . ?
Caution cancels love's richer part; eros,

sequestered in home safety, always seems
to die by inches. The house wins by turning
its people into furniture. Many tombs

are made of unplayed cards. It's me I'm warning
here. Hit when the asking happens. The house
may have its system, but you're not through learning.

INSTRUCTIONS

A rich voice inside a dream
gave instructions for the return of breath.
I learned of the burning pain the no-longer
dead endure as sunken lungs reinflate,
the heart like a rheumatic hand fists limply
and fingers in their cramp twitch again.

The voice urged caution. Waking cells
and neural circuitry, it said, are flooded first
with sadness, the steeped sum of a life's hurts,
reverses, botched choices with their compound interest,
their mortgage of sorrow. That dawn is like the
return from long stupor of a failed suicide.

Many in that onslaught will wish their oblivion
renewed. Yet joy, the voice pursued, returns too —
although for each cinematic sex-thrill or
palm tree package tour, there will be waves
of smaller graces not glimpsed at the time,
still ledgered in the mind's deeps, the body

in its flesh-alertness logged them all:
guava taste of a licked stamp for a phone bill
how many times unnoticed; cyan blue
of an idling laptop screen (like the colour
of ether, or taste of gin); the rounded vowels
of the mourning dove, concealed as if the June

greenery itself were singing (noticed once,
yet neglected) — all brimming now, all returned,
the voice urged, from the soul's cistern, or
was I the one speaking, I wondered, guiding
the voice, I hoped not, though at that moment
I woke up and remembered.

DREAM

I know I am in a dark place because I

       cannot swallow, and the wasps

are weaving hives

       into the dead eyes

              of the streetlamps

AN ACQUAINTANCE

(and one I'll never touch) but just now made this
lush, familiar love with, in sleep, summer
dawn fragment or phantasm, warmer though than
    any waking flesh, if I happen

to see you today or weeks on in the street
it'll be with this same shy fever, coming back to me
how rushed we were, and furtive — shades
    fading in each other's arms —

as if knowing how soon I would wake and end this,
    wholly against my will.

THE PEACE OF HIGH PLACES

Her map shows the bottomlands where deer drink rain,
the dredge ponds healed over by slow
films of time-lapse ice,
and sad, seasonal bungalows
on the ridge-rim of town, closed down
for winter, pipes drained,
beds cold —

Among juniper and stripped willow scrub
cranberries spring from cheechako graves
in the still chillness so beloved by hunters
and also by their game.

The lost sun has left its light in the fruit
and the eye in love always seeks in the heathery
groundcover mossed removes where any two
might lie together, somehow.

Her map shows the bottomlands where
deer drink rain, cupped in leaf loam
or hollowed lobes of granite,
and a fleeting refuge
on the city's ridge-rim, closed down
for winter, pipes drained,
bed cold —

PRAYER OF THE BURNT-OUT CASE

Nobody stuffs the world in at your eyes.
— Margaret Avison

"Clarify me like a mourne on Skye, or a seacliff
in the Cyclades — calm faces of bone-bleached limestone
contemplating seas without judgement, or cerebral
vivisection — cut through me only with the febrile
summer sun, to cells' answering suns, scorch away each foolscap
layer of brain like a winter bulb in root-cellar gloom,
    decades down
to where the midmost clove still glows,
specular as an eye, Zen as a fist ——

"Bear me up into light, all the light
that nerves can bear, I want to suffer
such luminous urgencies, awe of Lazarus whose hardened eyes
hatched open to the passed world's daggering beauty:
his pure-again first-seeing, and knowing
that he saw.

"Refine me to a stubborn last scut of land,
scoured headland in the Cyclades, or Hebrides, beacon
smashed blind and finally seeing, now the light
that hid night from the keeper is gone.
Or a desert — deserts in the lap of the sun.
Grind me new lenses from the desert sand."

THE LOST FRIEND AND CHILD HAD
THE SAME LOVELY NAME

by his own hand

A dream the night I got the news, that earlier
little item: dreaming beers on a basement couch
with D on the floor alongside, head slouched,
dead-still, till I lean over sling my arm over his shoulder

and tell him, D. Goodbye. He hears, his whole body now
quaking and he sobs, head lower, and I kneel
and say it again: So long. In some dreams how purely you *feel*
till morning kicks in and then just: anger, sometimes. Times now,

traitor, I want to tell him, call him, going over
to the other side, and by your own will, a turncoat,
tipping the scales, so that the dead ones further out-
weigh us. The rest of your life stillborn. Love's hoarder,

you've fallen into your own pockets, D, fallen back
into your own sockets, you're gone and did still
owe us more: words. (The owing was mutual
though: so we're quits.) And if the cloudwaters break

on mourners below, they might not add tears — might not
bother with the standard offerings, D, they're broke
and you stiffed them, I'm telling you they won't. You
    chose this — fuck,
you wanted this, D. They say you did.
                            I don't.

SHE'S

an alchemist of "the envious
practice of written speech," and I envy her,
every song an alembic fulminating
with fabulous constituents: liquid pewter, the jewelled
plumage of the hummingbird, pure laudanum
of flowing iambs. Those scorpions in their sepulchres
of resin: samphire and the friend-
killing heroin: her pen
brims over like a syringe with
elegies, torch songs, her tongue
like the arc-flame of the refiner
annealing the dead, still-anguished eyes
of a friend, into grace, or the base-
metal of our half-
murdered language:
                        now rejoined.

A WORD-DREAM IN WARTIME

16/11/01, 5:20 a.m.

The flesh is soft like paraffin,
the skin a body bag, stocked
with two-bit lobes and sacs: sacral loci
of quantum insight and orgasm, odes,
madrigals, fratricidal rage,
and Jesus never saved —

When slug frag shard or dum-dum stammer into flesh
they never talk straight but instead
loop and spool in fractals, or like stunt-show
pilots skywriting over the Ferris wheels and gunshot galleries of the Ex
maiming enough for a dozen deaths
   the way the addict's treasury of sedatives
   the way a bluffside of boulders
   romping down onto the hermit's hutch must both settle
   for less than they could take, and
   having the power to kill in spades
   be sated with just a single death
   (as if any death is a single death!) and
   Krishna never saved —

"I find the flesh," they murmur (these sly, sharp
tokens, as if for timeless subways of stalled,
flagged coffins), "soft
like paraffin"
    and the reliquary of the ribcage
a very partial armour
as if it would not do to protect the heart from everything,
these rifts and fissures a necessary wager,
and Allah never saved —

THE SHADOW BOXERS

Each year more of your life lost to shadow.
Small hours, blown open, blare with the soundtrack
of your hindsight, faces framed in the Prado
of memory seem realer than your son's, wisecracks
of an ex-ex-something outstabbing the actual
damage of sprain or wound. So it starts again,
night's neural colloquy, the patient quarrel
exhumed, ex-rival you again cross-examine

and now it's you there in the dock as the court's
night attorney mocks all your explanatory
gab (what you really meant, what you worry
she heard) — you and all sworn desperadoes
of the backward glance: self-held prisoners
in the mind's shrinking cell, battling shadows.

PROMISED LAND

Lonely as a motel mirror, or the crop-dust
winds at dusk, down a highway in the West
on the high plains the day daylight saving dies
and you in the gravel by the car for a piss;

or is it the cold bulb-lustre that's cast
on a gutted phone booth, nights, beside the ghost-
grocery of some Badlands town; or was your loneliness
more a sound, a scent — hair-smells fading by the day from a
    towel, until only the faintest guess?

Still it was good then, wasn't it, that feeling, each wave
like a hit that hurt you deeper into the world, to lift you off feet
    like a line
of early Springsteen, "madman drummers," and you roaring
    along with the black spinning tire of the LP, *I believed* all
    the saxophone

backstreets Clarence Clemons riffed off would keep belting out
    miles beyond Main
with Kerouac on rip-rap rhythm apace, a summons beyond law,
    till the heart in hard solitary could only hammer out *I believe,*
I believe, I believe — and you really did. And I do: nights still,
                                                    believe.

ULTRASOUND

As in water face answers to face,
                                   so here —
full moon awash in the autumn
waters of the lake
in the last, late ferry's wake
answers to the moon's face: pale madonna. And you —
wavery shape in the still, unbroken
waters of the womb, how you blink
upward into the world — still blurred —
you gazing as if intent to see out, to find
that lone, beloving face
that peers down, suckles you with first and
perfect light, then draws you,
tidal, into the world.

RAVINES

Summers the ragweed empty lots
and the schoolfields in green fever
HAVE YOU SEEN THIS CHILD?
                                    I've seen her,
a daughter,
hair soft as the silk of milkweed

who was absent years until the eye
tired, bleared with finding then losing her
over and over in the face of a stranger's child
A woman felt this
in a bus shelter winter rain veined, postered
with dated grade-school snaps, each caption
a love poem of stats, inconsolable
particulars
HAVE YOU SEEN THIS CHILD?
                                    I have,
I still remember —

Remember a dream where you watch the bereft ones
filing down into a basement flat, in cinder-
block projects along the Humber,
to petition the shrugging collector, mayor
of the underground, while in the docklands
or ravines slashed green by the Don, others
are calling out *Koré*
Koré

        there is no loss unless you are gone
        there is no love until this one

Only Koré's face
through summer, when the fields in green fever

flourish and burn, a daughter, born and found,
with her eyes twinned tarns,
hair soft as the silk of milkweed —

DESERT PSALM

As thermals at sunrise draw swallows in geysers out of the dead
    mouths of abandoned mines, as if birds were the desert's
    address to the sky and earth's inner anthem embodied
Let these words lift that same way
Anew

As the pure, potent mescal of the sunrise courses toward me
    over the mesa to rejuvenate the fading Marada
Let these words light and linger on the right things
    rivering that same instinctive way
Anew

NEWS FROM ANOTHER ROOM

Back in a moment with more coverage of America's new war!
— CNN, 09/14/01

This is simple as simple comes. He refills
your wine glass before you can argue.
There are no "new wars," only episodes
of that same crude, ancestral fever.
But every love's a new thing — feels it — knotted,
frail collaboration. Fill his glass
with those deeper lees.
The foghorn, rusting of rain on park heroes,
low vespers of a glacial river all
give news enough for now. Refill his
mouth with the warm red wine
of your tongue, this is simple
as simple comes.

IV

FIFTEEN APPROXIMATIONS

Every poem is a failed translation.

— Robert Kroetsch

THE DRUNKEN BOAT

(Arthur Rimbaud, 1871)

I flowed with the Rivers' incurious currents,
no longer guided by any boatmen ashore;
whooping savages had nailed them all naked
to totem poles and transformed them into targets.

I was unmoved, cared nothing for any crewmen,
or cargoes of Flemish wheat or English cotton —
now the crowd ashore were finished with their howling
the unreined Rivers let me go where I wanted

and so in the furious lashings of last winter's
tidal bore, deaf as a stubborn child, I was free.
No slab of the bank broken loose by those waters
could have revelled in a more triumphant spree!

At sea, storms hallowed my night-watches with joy;
lighter than a cork I danced over waves known
as the unceasing rollers of drowned men, ten
nights, never missing the vapid eyes of the quay-

lanterns in port. Sweet as the tart flesh of green
apples to a child, the salt water seeped through my
pinewood hull, rinsed splotches of vomit and cyan wine
clean off me, tore my anchor and rudder away.

And ever since that time I've bathed in the poem
of the sea, steeped and milky with stars, guzzling
the green azures, where at times the ecstatic flotsam
of a drowned man, pale and pensive, will be sinking;

where, dyeing the sudden blueness, deliria,
slow rhythms under the blood-light of day, stronger
than liquor, louder than your lyres, the bitter
rednesses of love ferment! I know how lightning

cracks the skies, know the waterspouts, the undertows
and currents, I know the evenings and how dawn
erupts from the sea like a rabble of doves;
at times I've seen what people only dreamed they saw!

I saw the low sun, poxed with mystical horrors,
lighting, in long violet swaths of seeming calm
(like brightly robed actors in classical dramas),
the far roll of waves like a mill's shuddering oars.

I dreamed of green nights with dazzled snows, slow
kisses rising to the water's eyes before rest,
the circulation of astounding saps, the gold
and blue wakings of melodic phosphorescence.

I heard for months the surging of the sea's battery
against reefs, like the roars of a penned, crazed herd,
never dreaming the luminous feet of the Marys
could muzzle up the lowing, broken-winded surf.

I ran aground on Floridas, those incredible
coastlines whose flowers conceal panther-eyed men;
where rainbows stretched out as taut as a bridle
mingle with glaucous flocks under the skyline.

I saw immense marshes putrescing, saw snares
where Leviathan rotted among reeds; the sea's
doldrum face agape like a chasm, vistas
collapsing into the far, cataracting bays.

Glaciers, silver suns, pearly waves and embering
skies, groundings at the far end of murky lagoons
where enormous serpents, beset by vermin,
flop from twisted trees in whiffs of black perfume.

I would have liked to show children the dorados
in the blue combers, those golden fishes, those singing
fishes . . . Blown seaward I was cradled by flowers
of spindrift, while winged by ineffable winds.

Tired martyr of meridians and zones! Often
the sea whose sobs were the source of my rolling
would buoy toward me yellow-belled shadow blossoms
while I remained still — a weary woman, kneeling.

Like an island at large, I hosted on my sides
the squabbles and the guano of the gulls, eyes blond,
sailing on while seamen through my frail knot-lines
sank supine to their slumber with the drowned.

Now I, a boat lost in the seaweed hair of bays
or hurled by hurricanes into birdless ethers;
whose brine-drunk carcass not even the Monitors
nor Hansa merchants could have managed to raise;

who was free and afire, crowned with violet mists,
masts piercing the heavens turning red like a wall
with sunset's shining lichens and the azure snots
of the sky, sweet preserve of the great poets; hull

rushing, splashed with electric new moons, insane
and driven plank, with a black seahorse escort,
when July with bludgeon blows made the ultramarine
skies implode into cyclones; hull atremble, alert

from sea-miles off to the heaving, groundswell groans
of rutting Behemoths and the turbid maelstroms. . . .
I, eternal cruiser of immovable blues,
finally miss Europe's ancient walls and dams!

Archipelagos of stars, islands whose fevered skies
fan open to all mariners — perhaps it's in these
deep-fathomed nights you sleep in refuge, my
lost strength, like untold gold birds, to arise someday?

But it's true, I've wept too much. The dawns tear my heart.
Every sun is bitter, every moon is cruel.
Love has swollen and slowed me with inebriate
torpors . . . if only my keel would crack and my hull

rupture, let me sink! If I still long to float
on Europe's waters, it's a small pool, black and chill
in the fragrant dusk, where a stooped and sorrowful
child is letting go his butterfly-frail boat.

Steeped in the languor of your waves I can no longer
track the wide wake of the cotton-bearing steamer
or challenge the pride of the flagship, the warship,
or scull under the prison-ship's terrible eyes.

LE VAISSEAU D'OR

(Emile Nelligan, 1903)

It was a huge ship, hewn out of solid gold,
whose sails grazed the clouds over unknown seas;
its figurehead, with hair blown back, breasts bold,
arched high at the bow through the blaze of the days.

But one night it ran aground on a massive reef
in the dissembling ocean, sirened with wind,
and the terrible foundering that brought it to grief
filled the sea's coffers, where it lies now, coffined,

still. It was a gold ship whose diaphanous hull
was a window on troves of loathing, madness, disgust,
and on the crewmen competing to hoard the most

in their drowning. What's left of it, in the lull
after the beating storm? And my heart — what has become
of that ghost ship? Gone — sunk in the gulfs of a dream.

THE SLEEP AT SEA

(Homer, The Odyssey, *Book 13, lines 76–93)*

Now the crewmen sit to their oars in order and slip
the cable from the bollard hole and heave backwards
so their oarblades chop at the swell and churn up water
while over Odysseus sweet sleep irresistibly
falls so fathomless and sound it might almost be the sleep
of death itself. And the ship like a team of stallions
coursing to the crack of the lash with hoofs bounding
high and manes blown back like foam off the summits of waves
lunges along stern up and plunging as the riven
rollers close up crashing together in her wake
and she surges on so unrelenting not even a bird
quick as the falcon could have stayed abreast. . . .
So she leaps on splitting the black combers bearing
a man godlike in his wisdom who has suffered years
of sorrow and turmoil until his heart grew weary
of scything a path home through his enemies or the furious
ocean; but now he sleeps profoundly, with all his griefs,
asleep at his side, forgotten.

THE MOVER

(Valerio Magrelli, 1992)

"What is translation?" On a platter
the pale, flaming head of a poet.
                            — Nabokov

The mover who means to
clean out my room is doing
the same job as me. I
too move something — words —
to a new building, words
not mine, setting hands to things
I don't quite know, not quite
comprehending what I move.
Myself I move — translate
pasts to presents, to presence, that
travels sealed up, packed in pages, or
within crates bearing the inscription
FRAGILE. Don't know what's in them. And
this is what the future holds —
this shuttling, the metaphor, the tense
and manual grammar,
the transfer, the figure
of speech, the moving-
company come to move you.

VOWELS

(Arthur Rimbaud, 1871)

Black A, white E, red I, green U, blue O — vowels,
someday I'll disclose your undiscovered births.
A: black hairy corset of flies that burst forth
to spin and buzz above shadow-gulfs and cruel

stenches. E, blank frankness of mists and pavilions,
proud glacial spires — white kings — quivering umbel.
I, violets, a junkie's red spit, gape of ample
lips laughing in rage or in drunken contritions;

U, arcs, divine vibrato of viridian seas,
the peace of creaturely pastures, the furrows
that study inscribed in the alchemist's features;

O, the final trumpet, charged with strange stridors,
silences spanned by archangels and galaxies,
and O, Omega — the violet beams from her eyes! —

HAPPENS A MAN

(Rainer Maria Rilke, 1903)

Happens a man will stand up from his supper
and walk out his door, and walk, and walk,
because a church is waiting in the east somewhere;

and his children bless him as if he were dead.

And another who does die, and in his own house,
remains there, trapped in his pipe and his clock,
so his children must venture to the east instead

to find the church that their father forgot.

IN SPARTA

(after Ángelos Sikelianós, 1943)

I've had my eye on you, as if in ambush —
a lame, toothless wolf. Out of the fast scrum
it's you I've settled on, your face and flesh
the ones that most appealed. (Not that way.) Come,
let me take your shoulder, guide you — as if led
by the bit and harness — upstairs. This one night
you'll deepen my feeble imprint in the bed
and lie in her arms, your feet between her feet.

She's slender, my love, petite as Helen — still,
I want you to fill her with your seed. This hour
you'll keep her in your clasp (vital as mine was,
once) and . . . the rest you know. Give me a son for
Sparta's ranks. Then go. Please. I hope you will —
give me something for my age. Before death does.

See Plutarch's *Life of Lycurgos:* "*The aged husband of a young woman
could if he chose introduce her to a good, virtuous, handsome young man
whom he admired; and would deem the offspring of their coupling his
own.*"

LIKE A MAN

(Catullus)

Enough of this useless moping, Catullus,
it's over, write it off. Back then
when she was yours, the sun always shone
and you were on her like the sun,
insatiable, as she was, and she'll
never have it so good again.
Always at her heels, her side, or
inside her, Catullus, and that was
fine, whatever you wanted she wanted
and the sun — there's no denying it —
always shone.
                Now she's changed, gone cold,
and you'll have to be the same —
not pitiful, like this, no whiner, idler,
sorry stalker, tavern fixture.
Take it like a man. So here's so long.
When Catullus makes up his mind, girl,
that's it. He won't come haunting
your doorway, nights, like love's hunched
beggar . . . but then again, who will?
Your nights will be as cold as his!
How will that suit you for a life?
Who'll come to see you then? Who
flatter you on your looks, give you
what he gave you all the time, and
take you around, kiss you,
be your fan? And you, girl —
who are *you* going to kiss,
yes, and bite . . . ?
                Ah, Catullus,
enough, you know it's over.
And you're taking it like a man.

PYRRHA

(Horace)

What slender elegant youth, perfumed
among roses, is urging himself on you,
  Pyrrha, in the fragrant grotto? Have you
    bound your yellow hair so gracefully

for him? How many times he'll weep because
faith is fickle, as the gods are, how often
  will the black, sea-disquieting winds
    astonish him, although for now

credulous, grasping at fool's gold, he enjoys you,
hopes you'll always be calm water, always
  this easy to love. Unconscious of the wind's wiles
    he's helpless, still tempted

by your gleaming seas. But high on the temple wall
I've set this votive tablet, and in thanks
  to the god for rescue have hung
    my sea-drenched mantle there.

THE BURN

(Jean Takamura, 1972)

She was somebody else while I burned
and didn't know. Gut ground-fires
either die out or they kill you; either way
you're through. But her salving fingers
found me in time. Now I need to know
if, while I burned
alone, she did somewhere too.

And while I slept badly, did she sleep?
I see her aboard night trains
and charter flights, bound for some vital
meeting, or morning session, lines
in her face in the first sunlight
piercing sleep
and my shoulder aches at the weight

of her head there, as if it was there,
then. Here she is with me tonight
and her ghost still haunts me. Into her body
these longer, desperate thrusts, as if to root
myself in her depths, find passage through
to all her elsewheres
the way she's now lodged in mine — although

seemingly with no effort or concern.

And so in this new way I burn.

MY MARROW FLAME

(after Sappho)

He is not a hero, he is more
a god in my eyes, that man
who sits beside you, the one

close enough to hear each separate
word — your words — him lost in the pure
canto of your voice, the pour

and splash of laughter that makes my
blood bound fast. And when suddenly
I meet you, I can make no sound, my

tongue is helpless and my marrow
flame, my skin ablaze, I see
nothing and I hear no more

than the flood in my ears, that hard
drumming, as I drip with sweat
and tremble. Then all the heat

drains from my skin and I fade
to frost, like winter grass.
                            Times like that I
feel death next to me —

TO THE LOVERS:

(from Dante's Inferno, *Canto V, 116–142)*

"Francesca, your suffering makes my heart
    the twin of yours, out of pity, sorrow — but tell me,
    in that time of sweeter sighing how did it start,

the love, when first it tendered longings that only
    conscience confined?" And she replied, "The hardest sorrow
    is to summon up, in times of sorrow, another, fiercely

joyful time, as your teacher, having cause to know,
    can attest. But if you're of a mind and have heart to hear
    of our love's first flowering, I will speak with the thorough

candour of one who speaks through tears. How, one day, for
    guileless pleasure, we read a story of Lancelot,
    caught in love. We were alone, unforeseeing, unaware,

and at times as we read aloud our glances met
    and our eyes locked and would not part and the avid
    colour in our faces drained. Then came the moment that

undid us: when Lancelot finally sees the vivid
    smile uncloud his lady's face, and gives her, bold in joy,
    a kiss. At these words another lover — the same, sad

one you see beside me, here, forever beside me,
    kissed my open lips, shuddering. Like a go-between that book
    and its author seduced us to our fall; that day

we read no further." All the while as Francesca spoke
    the second ghost beside her wept and sobbed; as if fierce
    pity could kill, I could feel my body growing weak

until I fell as a dying body falls.

THE SONG OF CH'ANG-KAN

(Li Bai)

With my hair still cropped across in bangs
I played, plucking flowers by the front gate.
You came trotting by on a bamboo horse
and we rode in make-believe around the echo well.
So we lived on in the village of Ch'ang-kan,
both sweet as green plums, free of guile.

At fourteen I became your wife,
so bashful my features stayed closed to you,
head turned down and away, unable to turn
and face you, though you called and called.

At fifteen I flowered open in smiles, yearning
to mingle my dust with yours;
so many times I promised you faith until death,
I had no use, then, for lookout towers.

A year later you left, took passage north
beyond the swirling rapids of Chu Tang Yen Yu
which no one dares traverse in the fifth month.
Overhead the monkeys make mournful chatter.

Now by the gate passersby come so seldom
green moss creeps over the steps, layered mosses
so deep I cannot clear them away, and leaves
stripped early by the autumn wind.

The butterflies brought by August
still flitter — two left — over grass in the west
garden. Their passing grieves me.
Waiting, I age.
            One day, if you come back, sailing down
through the brown narrows of the River Kiang,
and if you let me know in time,
to welcome you home I would go as far
as the ford at Cho Fu Sa.

LOVE, I AM GRATEFUL . . .

(Sappho)

that you're here, it was good
you came, I did need
to see you. You have made

love burst to flame inside
me, in my heart, may God
bless you, love you as hard

as the hours have seemed
endless to me and sad
since we parted —

UNDER A BAD STAR

(Charles Baudelaire, 1861)

To raise up a weight as heavy as that
would take a Sisyphus, demand a heart
that bold, and even if you did have heart
for the work, well — Art is long and the hour late.

Far from the pompous, famous tombs
toward a potter's field lonely and apart
my heart, like a torn and muffled drum,
goes beating, beating its funeral march.

How many jewels sleep sheathed in the earth
in black oblivion, beyond the depth where
miners burrow with their bores and their drills;

many a flower will reluctantly share
the long-withheld secret of its smells
with the senseless waste-places of the earth.

"The American Night Listens": The reference in line 10 is to actor Jack MacGowran's great reading of Beckett's fiction on the Cladagh LP *MacGowran Speaking Beckett*. The poem's first two lines are from a dream.

"Mixed Tapes," lines 11–12: The unnamed singer I have in mind here is Bryan Ferry.

"The Last Living Speaker of the Erondha Tongue . . ." is for David O'Meara.

"Promised Land" is for Michael Holmes.

"Ultrasound" is for Graeme Balint and his amazing family.

"Ravines": *Koré* is Greek for "daughter" (modern Greek: Κόρη, pronounced KOree). In some versions of the myth, Demeter, in search of Persephone, wanders the world calling out this word.

"Like a Man": My approximation of this poem owes something to Louis Zukofsky's version (see *Latin Poetry in Verse Translation*, edited by L. R. Lind, HMCO, 1957).

"The Song of Ch'ang-kan": For this approximation I'm indebted to Gary Geddes for his fine and faithful (compared to Ezra Pound's great and unfaithful) translation.

ACKNOWLEDGEMENTS

It would take me too long to shorten the list — the address book, almost — of people whose poetry, conversation, and other generosities have helped in the writing of these poems. But here I want to thank those who have actually seen several of the poems or translations and offered criticism. Thank you Suzanne "Sparky" Buffam, Mary Cameron, Tim Conley, Judith Cowan, Lynn Crosbie, Heather Frise, Michael Harris, David Helwig, Stephen Henighan, Iain Higgins, Christine Klein-Lataud, Claudia Valeria Letizia, David Manicom, Una McDonnell, George McWhirter (for suggesting José Emilio Pacheco's term "aproximaciónes" for my translations, both faithful and free), Andy Patton, Michael Redhill, Ingrid Ruthig, David Staines, John Unrau, and Chris Wiseman. Special gratitude goes to Ken Babstock, Michael Holmes, and Jay Ruzesky; also to Don McKay — the notorious UncleLear — who edited these poems with care and insight, and prevented several ornithological bloopers. Thank you Mary, you especially. And my father, John Heighton, and my sister, Pelly. Thanks are also due (again) to Bill Douglas and my wonderful, tough publisher, Martha Sharpe.

I'm grateful also to the editors of the following magazines and anthologies where some of these poems first appeared, in earlier versions: *Arc*, *Books in Canada*, *BRICK*, *Canadian Literature*, *The Common Sky*, *The Fiddlehead*, *Letting Go*, *Leviathan Quarterly* (UK), *Lichen*, *Malahat Review*, *Matrix*, *New Quarterly*, *nth position* (online), *PRISM international*, *Quarry*, *Queen Street Quarterly*, *subTERRAIN*, *Writers' Forum* (UK), *Written in the Skin* and *The Yalova Festival Anthology* (Turkey).

"Address Book" won first prize in the 2001 Petra Kenney poetry awards, London, England. My thanks to founder Morgan Kenney.

"Mixed Tapes" appeared as above/ground press broadsheet #189, Nov. '03. Thanks to publisher Rob McLennan.

Finally, I'd like to acknowledge the important support of the Canada Council for the Arts; the Ontario Arts Council; the Concordia University English Dept., which gave me a writer-in-residence position during the 2002–03 school year; and the Pierre Berton House Foundation, Whitehorse, Yukon. Thank you so much.